Sitting on a Sunny Cliff

*Unpolished Poetry by
Jake Jones*

Copyright © 2025 Jake Jones

Photographs © 2025 Luner Rey

Photographs on pp 8, 12, 28, 38, 42, 52
© 2025 Lewis Photographs

All rights reserved.

ISBN: 978-1-7394806-3-9
ISBN10: 1-7394806-3-5

Contents

Doorway Dog 7

Enough? 9

Departure 11

Hang the pictures high 13

The Mother 15

The Birds 17

A Different Knock 19

I will wait 20

No carrots for Rudolf 21

How will you leave? 23

It hasn't hit me yet 25

Judge me? 27

Sitting on a sunny cliff 29

Freedom 30

Breakdown 31

The Silent Man 33

Forget me not	35
What you looking at?	37
Stairs	39
There's nothing that compares	41
Fire all the bullets	43
OCD	45
Death Bed	47
Speak?	48
I don't need ID	49
I know?	51
Anything you wanna do babes!	53
Get It Honey	55
One-Man Army	56
Just a poet	57
Adfam	60
About the Author	61

Doorway Dog

We will be together side by side,
Even when I'm scared and have no place to hide,
I watch the brightlights while he takes a nap,
I feel nice and safe in my owner's lap,
Sometimes he gets tired but that's okay,
I get stroked by passersby throughout the day

But this time he slept even more,
Hunched over on the cold hard floor,
I will wait and wait – he's my only thought.
Then came Brightlights of a different sort,
I watch him be taken away,
In comes the darkness, here comes the rain.

Shoes on the pavement, a shadow in the way
"Hey little fella what's your game"
I raise my nose to the voice and into the black I say
"I am the doorway dog, the dog with no name"

Enough?

This is not enough
Walking to the end, but not the end of the night
Air foggy as I stay in the gaze of sight
The same looks from the night before are thrown
As I stand so very much on my own
As I stand and wait for my fate
Another day where comfort comes late.

Counting coins, I hear a noise, assessing every shadow,
Fingers frozen feel the chill and the burn from old tobacco.

My day is finally done
The long awaited time has come.

As I hold it up to the light,
This won't last me through the night.
This is not enough.

Departure

Breakdown
Barriers
The wrong track

Faces blurred

Signs

Signals
Messages

Anticipation of plans
The rumble of release
Please, Mind the gap
Step out, step off

Hang the pictures high

Looking through unfinished albums on how our lives used to be
The work around the house was meant for you, we would always agree.

So, I hang the pictures high where it was just empty space
I hang the pictures high to liven up the place
I will open up the curtains so the sun shines on you its gaze
I will decorate you with tinsel on a lonely Christmas Day
I might not always remember the words you used to say
So, I hang the pictures high in pride of place.

I hang the pictures high for all to see
You reply with a smile while I make just one cup of tea.

I will talk with you until the walls fall down
Then rebuild them with my old weathered hands.

So hang the pictures high
Watch them age
Remember all the good old days.
Now it's my time to go.

The pictures will show how I loved you so
So hang my picture next to yours
Around the person I adore.

Stand at the wall and you will see
That there's a place for you and a place for me
Adding till eternity
On the great wall of family.

The Mother

The breakfast was arranged in the usual way
And at the normal time so as not to cause distress
She heard the excited footsteps
Of not one but two feet coming down the stairs
The glowing pair entered the room with an almost seeable connection
His new 'friend' was introduced and the pair quickly sat down
and got into conversation

As she looked at her son
The mother saw what the medication could not cure
And what her love could not give
As he sat there chatting at the breakfast table
He poured the milk for her with such care, yet confidence and grace
As his wit flowed so natural and deep
The normal routine now seems as if it could never've worked
As she stares at her grown up son
Something not felt and seen before

She lets it unfold

The Birds

The birds talk to me, I just heard my name,
Flying up so high they will not be tamed,
Not scared of the creature,
but of what it can say,
Can you work out what the chirps convey?

A coincidence too many times,
The same bird 'song', line after line,
"Twit, twit, twit, it's you"
I can hear the voices,
Can you hear them too?

Flaps in my ear, then the noise disappears,
They follow me everywhere I go,
Tune into the tune of the predictions of doom,
Then life will go more with the flow,

The chirps of threes and fives,
Tell me how to live my life
Pecking at my brain in a rhythmic way
Make sure you listen to what they have to say

But now I know they're coming for you!
The birds told me and they will tell you too...

A Different Knock

A different knock to the door,
words are not needed no more.

Send the kids out to play,
for they will not return children today.

No need for pen nor paper to write the date,
take away the empty plate.

Hear a silence not heard before,
as you close the microwave door.

Thoughts that never leave your head,
say goodnight to the empty bed.
Tomorrow will echo the same refrain—
the start of the quiet, endless pain.

I will wait

I lost you once before but now I will never leave your side
Now I'm there for every birthday and every time you have cried

I waved you away on your first day at school
I told you that boy was a fool

I was there when you thought I wasn't
and with you when you thought I was

Together we chose the bouquet
I walked with you down the aisle on your wedding day
I sit with you and watch the grandchildren play

Now it is your time
Your spirit leaves you as you climb
You smile and pass me as you shine
As you disappear, I will have no fear
Because a smile from you is all I need
To last me till eternity

No carrots for Rudolf

She opens up the fridge on a cold Christmas Eve
Stands on tippy toes but no carrots can be seen
Opens up the milk that smells green and strange
No milk for Santa on tomorrows Christmas Day

No decorations, the walls look bare and grey
She tries to open the jar of cookies, that have been locked away

Its so hard to sleep she prays and prays,
Praying for presents on Santa's sleigh

No presents from Santa in her stocking makes it harder to believe,
No presents for her under the imaginary tree

How will you leave?

How will you leave? Better than before?
From the hub of emotions with many floors

Running through hallways of thoughts and silence
Starting to pray to a new God for guidance

Rearrange and arrange the vase of flowers,
Contemplate for hour after hour

Thinking back to when it was better –
This is the start of the pain that may last forever

Many stories incomplete or at the end
Will they lose a friend? Or fall in love again?

Some on their knees, some sleep on the floor,
The world for some not the same anymore

Hands clasped tightly, words unsaid,
Hopes for the living, tears for the dead.

Each day, the pages turn unseen,
The outcomes blurred, the meaning between.

So how will you leave? Better than before?
On which side will you be of the revolving door?

It hasn't hit me yet

I see others with heads bowed low,
Candles flicker, they feel the glow.
Their minds drift skyward, far from here,
Wrapped in the glow of something near.

It hasn't hit me yet
Staying here by the skin of my teeth,
I hope for a sign, and a sense of relief.
The candles flicker as more wine is poured,
I feel the need for something more.

I look to escape far from here,
Wrap me in the glow of something near.

It hasn't hit me yet,
But perhaps it will—
When the wine runs dry,
And the world stands still.

Judge me?

I entered again and did not hear
Not even a whisper not even a cheer

You didn't read it properly
Read it again
You don't know on what this depends

My prize is the silence
My mind the thing that shook.
Take away the fans and all that's left is the looks

You don't understand what's it's like to be me
I will show you and you will see

When I'm gone you'll see my fame
But you dashed it away, again and again

A light in my life slowly going dim
You could have saved me but you put me in the bin

So read my last entry and let it sink in
Because that is the one that will always win

Sitting on a sunny cliff

Sitting on a sunny cliff I can feel the breeze
I feel bigger than the mountains, stronger than the trees
The sun is now coming out on this cloudy day
The tracks are now connected for the train.

The engine will always need its coal
The ship is on its course because I patched up the hole
I took the honey and got a few stings
It's just what this life brings

But sitting on a sunny cliff it's a long way down
Part of me is here, but part is not around.
Like a broken umbrella in the rain
The tracks are now getting rusty from the train
Like the sun going away on cloudy days
I'm on the edge, and too close to the rays.

Freedom

At the school gates never late
Waiting, for his mates on a BMX,
checking his texts
No teacher tells him what to do
Lighting dad's cigarette too
A sense of freedom not known by many
Counting up pounds and pennies

They change to trainers on their feet
And march through the paths and the streets

After football and scraped knees
It's time for tea
Says his goodbyes, and lies thinking up plans for the rest
of the night
Back on the bike
As the lights close in
Feeling the cold wind, on his skin
Riding round still while others are in bed
Life and the rubber is losing its tread
Walking with his bike up the hill
But it's better than reality still

A sense of freedom not known by many
As the house the house feels cold and empty
Now counting just the pennies
A sense of freedom is plenty

Breakdown

Open cupboard
Get a cup
Close cupboard
Put cup down
Take the kettle
Turn on the tap
Open kettle lid
Fill the kettle
Turn off the tap
Close kettle lid
Put the kettle down
Switch on the kettle
Take a teabag
Put it in the cup
Wait for water to boil
Take kettle
Pour water in the cup
Put the kettle back
Open fridge
Get milk from fridge
Take off the cap
Close fridge
Pour the milk
Put on milk cap
Open fridge
Put in milk
Close fridge

Reach for sugar
Open sugar
Open drawer
Find a teaspoon
Spoon in sugar
Stir
Squeeze teabag
Take teabag out of cup
Open bin
Put teabag in bin
Put spoon in washing up
Pick up cup

Drink

Relax

The Silent Man

The silent man came to me today
Said he had a lot to say
Said he would only speak to me
He needed to speak urgently

He already knew my name
Knew what I was going to say
Said that we are the same

He's got to tell me all he knows
Said he knew every pole
But didn't know, which way to go

He would make me feel so free
He said that they had mentioned me

He said,
"Don't listen to a word they say.
Stick with me and you'll be okay"
Said they wouldn't understand,
With a raised voice from the Silent Man

Now I see him everywhere
Both of us in despair
Said he couldn't trust me now
I must do
What he will choose
For the Silent Man.

Forget me not

When life has lost its meaning
And it's me that makes you cry
Chain me not to life's old leaning
We will make it through somehow.

When the moonlight reaches its hour
When the cold fog starts to lay
If you find it's me you're missing
Just know I will return

Forget me not
For I am honest
Save me not
From the truth
I'm within, just unspoken
I'll return to you somehow

If you find it's me you're missing
If you're hoping I'll return
Just you know I'm always listening
Know that I will return

When the task seems to outweigh us
When it all seems lost and gone
Forget me not
Forget my demons
I'll return to you somehow.

Forget me not
For I am honest
Save me not
For I am honest
Save me not
From the truth
When I reach, reach my calling
I'll return to you somehow.

What you looking at?

"I've got a mate – he knows karate"
"Well, I've got a mate – he's in the army"

"I've been learning origami – don't get me wrong
I'll fold your head into a paper swan
You don't have the minerals to take me on"

"Don't you know who my dad is?"
"Well my dad used to drink with Reggie Kray"
"What did you say?"
"I said my dad used to drink with Ronnie Kray"

"I'd be careful if I was you. My cousin's Big David"
"What big 'big' David, that's crazy – we must be related"

"Come on – you can buy me a kebab
And have you got a spare fag I can nab?"

Stairs

Walking up a set of stairs to get back to the top
Sometimes it's easy
Sometimes it's not

One's head can make it a mountain to climb
By new situations you don't usually find.

Walking up with courage will protect you from the drop
Walking up with knowledge will teach you it will stop.

You can wait but the stairs will never age
If not the whole set the just do one step per day

But remember all the other stairs have now gone and are behind
And that you will have the power within, the top at last to find

There's nothing that compares

There's nothing that compares
I get the warm glow
You're my only goal
It feels like you protect me from this world

You make me feel like me
Take me to places I've never been
Make me feel safe
You bring me up
Help me to sleep

There's nothing that compares to you
I can't get enough of you
All my time spent with you
Always waiting for you

Constantly on my mind
Only thing I wake up for
How will I do this?

It's over

Fire all the bullets

Fire all the bullets
Fix the bayonets
Assume the position
Break it off in the enemy's chest

Send all the missiles
Let the kids be scared
Hid in the bunkers
Til the death count is fair

Call every man and boy to fight
Don't stop til the fires burn bright

So, fire every bullet
It's the only way
For the wars to end this day

OCD

Organised chaos disorder

Again and again

The chaos of order

Again and again

Order, arrange

Its all the same

Arrange and arrange

Precise and aimed

The chaos disorder, of the orders order

Will order the orders to disorder

Order is, order is, order is, order,

Organised chaos disorder

Death Bed

Do not bring me my trophies for I will not win

Do not bring me a preacher for my simple sins

Do not bring me my weapons to try and fight the fear

Do not bring me tissues to wipe away my tears

Do not bring me money to try and buy more life

Do not sell your soul to make me feel alive

Do not change your world for me

This is how it's supposed to be

All that I really need

Is a room full of family

Speak?

What would happen if you couldn't speak for a day?
Would you miss all the things you would usually say?
Would you try to fight it and try to scream and shout?
Or listen to a friend and get them out and about?
With so many questions, wouldn't you reach your peak?
Or would you lock eyes and let your silence speak?
There will be those who speak for you,
But will you stand composed knowing the whole story?
But will you remember the silence?
The silence of glory

I don't need ID

Hello shopkeeper. I'd like to buy this 18 game
It will be great to enjoy after my hard job at the end of the day
I've just been at the pub to volunteer
Do you like my new Rosie and Jim tattoo I've had for years?

I don't need ID,
I know the code,
453470

My Legoland driving license will have to do,
I should have words with my lawyer about you

Take a look outside your see my car over there in the distance very, very far
My Dad's with me but he has a growing disease
and looks like he is in his teens

If you want shopkeepermate we can take this outside!
Just bring the game in a bag to hide

What if I was to tell you I've got 6 months to live?
That's not even enough time to get past the tutorial bit

Please let me buy it – I'll be your best friend
Cross my heart and hope to die till the bitter end

Looks like I'll have to take my business elsewhere,
I was going to invite you to my birthday party
But sorry life's not fair

I'll just go to a shop up the street
Get some fags and booze instead
Where I don't need ID

I know?

I know about the scar on the middle of your knee
I know sometimes you're shy, but can be the life and soul of the party
I know about Jane and John
I know about the instrument you put down and didn't carry on
I know there's a silver car outside in your street
I know you have a desire to be accepted by the people you meet
I know you had a great change around the age of 12
I know about the secrets you never tell

I know you've lived at a house with a number 2
Or maybe it was next-door
It's hard at the moment for the spirits to come through
Or maybe the house opposite in the road?
Anyway, you try to not complain or moan

But I know you will make a new friend
I know you will come into money to spend
This is a beginning of a new journey with another at an end
One thing for certain is that you'll be back again.

FISH &
CHIPS

Anything you wanna do babes!

We could hang around outside the chippy all day,
Anything you wanna do babes!
I would probably give you about a pound to spend
Or let's share a sausage and some crispy ends
Later we could go to the park
And smoke my dad's e-cig till it gets dark
I would show you some filthy drum and bass
And then try and kiss your orange face
I'll stay with you till I have to go in for tea
But I'll pick you up on my BMX at the gates at 3
I'll text you until my credit runs out
Then ask my mum for more as she screams and shouts

I know your speechless,
you don't have a lot to say,
But just remember, with me,
We'll do whatever you wanna do babes!

Get It Honey

As we say goodbye
God's hand takes you to the sky

As you reach the trees,
Make sure you bat the butterfly and bees

As you climb higher and higher where the birds flap,
when you get a second take a well-deserved nap

And while you are at Gods feet,
Make sure you ask him for a treat

But when you're with the guy,
Scratch him in the eye,
But leave one eye for me
Get it, Get it, Get it Honey!

In memory of Honey the cat

One-Man Army

Not allowed in Chequers,
Not allowed in Crowns
Not allowed in the Dancing Donkey
Or the Fox and Hound
I'm a one-man army
A marvel to be seen
Terrorising biddies
In Boughton-under-Blean
Call the parish council
I don't really care
As long as I have my Subaru to repair

Boxing on a Tuesday,
It's like human chess
I'm also a DJ
But I don't do requests

Take me or leave me
I'm that type of guy
Wear m' heart on my sleeve
I only speak my mind

Just a poet

I'm just a poet
Please don't beat me up
For all the sterotypical things I've written
And everyone I've slagged off

While you were practising punches
I was practising poetry
So please, please, please
Don't have a go at me

I'm sorry I made up a poem
Explaining how you're dumb
I'm sorry I made a poem up
About your mum

When you pick up that pen
You just can't put it down
It's a writer's thing
You just wouldn't understand

On second thoughts
I think that wasn't me
Sorry to the boy I plagiarised
Who lives down your street
If you really want, I can give you his address
He might act like he doesn't know
And probably won't confess

Actually, I'm not sorry
I'm the best Poet in the world
All you other writers
Write like little girls
Yeah – I said them things
It was me – then you'll see
'Cos I'm the best Poet
In the whole galaxy

A greater show of pain would have been if I hadn't written at all

Adfam is the leading families and addiction charity in England. We are here for all the millions of people affected by someone else's drinking or drug use. These people are children, parents, friends, partners, siblings and grandparents.

Coping with someone you love experiencing these problems can cause physical, mental, emotional, social and financial distress. Substance use or gambling are often just one part of the story – so many also suffer mental ill health, domestic abuse and financial problems.

They may be afraid to speak out so they are hidden in plain sight. Adfam gives them a voice. More than five million people are affected in this country and we know how tough it can be, so we want to make their lives better.

Our vision at Adfam is that family members affected by substance use or gambling are heard, valued and have access to support; that's why we do what we do.

www.adfam.org.uk

ABOUT THE AUTHOR

These poems probably give a good portrait of Jake, the poet. Things haven't been easy, but the journey has been interesting. He knows how to smile his way through, and he will always get there in the end.

Follow him on Insta: @jakejonespoet

Look him up on Facebook: @poetry-by-jake-jones

www.ingramcontent.com/pod-product-compliance
Lightning Source LLC
Chambersburg PA
CBHW060412080526
44583CB00012B/542